Collected Haiku
1997 - 2017

Other Books Of Poetry and Prose by Larry Kimmel

Betrayal On Maple Street (short stories)

Two Books: Branch after Branch
& As Far As Thought Can Reach

A Kind of Knowing
(conversations with spiritual healer, Floyd McAuslan)

As Far As Thought Can Reach (mini-essays, only)

a river years from here: haibun & poems

A Small Silent Ordeal (novel)

this hunger, tissue-thin

Blue Night & the inadequacy of long-stemmed roses

shards and dust

outer edges

thunder and apple blossoms (selected haiku 1997 - 2017)

Collected Haiku
1997 - 2017

Larry Kimmel

Stark Mountain Press
Colrain, Massachusetts

Collected Haiku 1997 - 2017
1ˢᵗ edition

Stark Mountain Press
364 Wilson Hill Road
Colrain, MA 01340

winfred@crocker.com
http://www.winfredpress.com

ISBN: 978-0-9864328-3-5

Images from Pixabay
Cover Design: Larry Kimmel

Acknowledgments

are due the editors of the following publications where these poems, sometimes in different form, first appeared: a motley sangha; Acorn; Atlas Poetica; black bough; bottle rockets; Bright Stars; Brussels Sprout; Cicada; Dasoku; dew-on-line; frogpond; Haiku Headlines; Ink, Sweat & Tears; LYNX; Mirrors; Modern Haiku; Moongarlic; NeverEnding Story; Nor' Easter; Northwest Literary Forum; Northwest Poetry Forum; Persimmon; Poetry in the Light; Point Judith Light; RAW NerVZ Haiku; Ribbons; HPNC Second International Rengay Contest 1996; short stuff; Simply Haiku; South by Southeast; still, *a journal of short verse*; The Christian Science Monitor; The Heron's Nest; The HNA Anthology 2001; The HNA Newsletter; The HSA Members Anthology 2007; The Nisqually Delta Review; The World Haiku Club; Timpieces 1997.

Dedicated to

new friends
&
old

————

When the Present has latched its postern behind my tremulous stay,
And the May month flaps its glad green leaves like wings,
Delicate-filmed as new-spun silk, will the neighbors say,
"He was a man who used to notice such things"?

> *from "Afterwards"*
> *Thomas Hardy*

———————

"I loaf and invite my soul ..."

> *Walt Whitman*

Introduction

Any reader who has read Larry Kimmel's, *the necessary fly* or *alone tonight*, will find many old friends in *Collected Haiku 1997 - 2017*, though often in different format. Still, there is a goodly number of haiku that have never been collected until now. *the necessary fly*, will be discontinued by the time this book is published, though *alone tonight* will remain in print, as *alone tonight* has a strong selection of tanka as well as a number of haibun besides the haiku. *Collected Haiku 1997 - 2017* represents all of the haiku that the author wishes to preserve at this time. A kind of twenty year haiku anniversary.

L. K.
Colrain, MA
December 2016

Collected Haiku
1997 - 2017

a screen door
bangs —

all past summers
summarized

in one brief
report

at Kate's Diner
under the plastic cake lid
— the necessary fly

in the spoon's
luster

the ceiling fan
pinwheels

wee and awry

the sticky sound of tires
on noontime asphalt –
      lemonade 10¢

no work today

even
with shutters
shut

the sun's
too loud

small rain ahead of storm –
a white butterfly crawls
under the Queen Anne's lace

long afternoon
a fly rides
the pendulum

on the rickety porch
painting her toenails cherry
also the dog's

stemless in the dusk
 the Queen Anne's lace float –
  the path grows luminous

on the porch
by moth light
we sit

not a word
between us

alone tonight
a moth taps
at the window

lying awake
   listening to the night sounds
   – white curtains billow

after a week
of roughing it – the bite
of hot water

this inch-sized frog traveling a foot each   leap

dead butterflies
    litter the road's edge . . .
        asphalt bubbles

a snake released –
the feel of it
stays in my hand ...

on the dusty dashboard
a daddy-longlegs, teetering

touch-me-nots
the big plump pod about to burst
– couldn't help myself

Queen Anne's lace
   right up to the door
      I've dated shorter women

dusk
and the daylily all but done

angry, but still . . .
asters
in an autumn breeze

in a gust

a red leaf
hops
from the curb

I catch it

brisk evening –

yellow jackets
too sluggish to leave the apple-drops

yellow leaves
at year's end

small griefs
haunt
my footsteps

November sunlight –
        its clear clean slant
                over threadbare pasture

gray blur
      breeze at my temple
            a gun shot cracks the evening air

the potted
shamrocks

are folded for
the night

two cups
of cocoa
steaming

on the cheek
of the brass
teapot

the embers'
cherry rouge

a bootstep
too near,

the kitchen cricket
quits

in mid-
December-
chirp

big soft snowflakes –
   seeing her smile
      I unbuckle my frown

      moonlight
      and the crunch of snow underfoot . . .
      her brown brown eyes

a chickadee
feeding
from my hand

the clutch
of tiny talons

snow falling falling
   through a claw of apple boughs
     – my failing mother

   empty branches strung with constellations

over glazed snow a spider crawling toward the end
    of February

the smell of soup in institutional halls
– the forced forsythia

muddy boots
everywhere the gurgle
of freshets

again today

I worked
on the *big* poem –

soon
there will be
crocuses

a grey
half-lidded
morning

the toast jumps
and I jump

in the woods
      the creek
            a cellophane endlessly crinkling

all over town
  turn signals flashing—here,
    spring peepers piping

where a dogwood
blooms
by a window

a sprinkle
of arpeggios

crabapple petals everywhere
I brush one
from her cheek

"Just look at the mud
   on your pants!"

in his fist
violets for her

maternity ward —
mine
the only home-picked
wildflower bouquet

a magnolia petal drops
in the morning chill
a young woman's taut blouse

in the park
a child brings me
a dandelion

in the park
under a sky
by Monet,
the girl
in the strawberry dress

vetch & yesterday's headlines —
the vacant lot nervous with squirrels

alone
I sip
espresso

two
sparrows court

tired from a day
    in the field, I close my eyes
        apple blossoms

looking up
looking down
dog
& llama
long & long

this snake –
  really not much more
    than a roving esophagus

where the small lake
leaks away . . .
a tea-dark gurgle

serpentine

the creek thrashes
having

swallowed
the
storm

tree cathedral
& me . . .
  church
  of
  one

midnight
say the prayer
take the pill

midnight
a whistler and his footsteps

if not
for the dripping
faucet –
alone
tonight

tOmatOes On the windOwsill sO red sO plump

after a day's debauch —
webworms webworms webworms webworms
along   an   evening   cherry   branch

                           k
at the string's end——the   n
                             o
                              t

    e x t e n d i n g   my lifeline with a scalpel

crossing the Piazza San Marco – me

One Tree Island

holding my eye as
she undoes her blouse –
my strict attention

an arch smile
then photons clothe her

wavelets lapping toes
the forest lake
there to receive her

wading out
till her breasts float
voices

diving under
a flash of bare bottom

she waves
from the one tree island
an exaltation of larks

———

in a shade of pines along the lake's edge
I clothe her
in a bikini of kisses

* * *

her number
not in my brain
but my finger

at the VFW
same scar
different story

in the brass
door knob
a distorted face

I grip
and twist

photo gallery
I've never seen eggs
look so nude

a coffee ring on my copy of Tolkien

where a fly butts & butts a windowpane the blank page

Sidewalk Café

sidewalk café
I tell the dog
'don't even think about it'

crumbs crumbs crumbs
is there anything
not crumbs

having refused the dog
I feed the sparrow
          – why?

a yellow jacket
circles my coffee mug
          – I wait

crumpled napkin
the sparrow's slight crouch
before take-off

* * *

first the model gets naked
then nude

she speaks
of her past –

on her face
the window prism's

iridescent bruise

in the hush
of the woods – something
she isn't telling

weeping
she
embraces me

the brook's
small babble

looking down
at the valley

I loaf
and let my mind

billow

over café au lait –

open-throated
laughter

and a perfume
you can taste

                              her face
                              anticipating
                              my words

                              an exaltation
                              of larks

sirens

a passing perfume
overwhelms

the smell
of
smoke

cicada afternoon –

in
the sanctuary's
coolness

stained-glass
parables

crossing the lawn barefoot
        arriving
              in dew time

Maple Street   my shady past

Cat & I

cat pushes glass figurine
a little . . . & a little . . . & . . .
ok, I get up

cat & I pretend she's hidden

cat comes
to an accordion stop
it's raining

it's raining
cat tries the back door

cat & I watch rain at open door

kitten runs up my jeans
& over my shoulder
I spill some water

* * *

spring breezes open nightgowns

thunder and apple blossoms
her naked presence in the orchard grass

a bare midriff – that's all it takes

stuck
for an answer

I lower
my eyes –

her ten
red
toenails

afterwards

through
an open window

the hot scent
of pine

evening settles
        on the patio
                a dusky lingerie
                        still warm

her diary —
if only I hadn't forced its tiny lock . . .

she's been here
and gone . . . the gift
of her perfume

the restlessness of leaf shadows on a crimson couch

turning
from the window

her blouse
full of sunshine
and shadow

I stick with the
weather

the erotic jive
in her eyes

shuts
down

back home
willing to fix the argument
for sex

lust
over the kitchen table
a 60 watt bulb

pussywillows
behind
the Court House

the smart click
of high heels

shaking
the stone from
her shoe

a white opal
swings

from between
brown breasts

she loiters
    smelling a spray of violets
    – the nape of her neck

from a high branch
an oriole holds forth –
green tea in white cups

stuck

on the blond curl
of the flypaper

a buzzing triad

in the sprinkler's rainbow
a wasp loses
              altitude

after a hard look –
    the copperhead flowing
        into the stones

another scorcher
  powder-fine dust
    on the roadside ragweed

a cow's bleached skull —
  in the cranium
      a paper wasp's nest

first cicada
one long sizzling syllable says it's summer

rolling a spruce needle
between thumb and finger
– harvesting the scent

storm tossed
poplars . . . if only
she'd phone

watching the loggers work
I rub my paper cut

frost-starred window –
I stare through my reflection
into the moonlit orchard

a dusting of snow
the chickadees's cluttered cuneiform

our fingers
touch
the small
arithmetic
of coins

clasping my dad's hand
    as once he gripped his father's hand
        whose hand had once . . .

after his stroke
a safety razor –
                    the strop still hangs
                    by the door

in all but one room
a death –
Victorian homestead

on the wall
where I live
a watercolor of home

in a shaded spot
the ruins
of a sundial

in the cool of the breathless cavern breathless

sunrise
three raps of a hammer
sunrise

with barbed wire
deep
in their guts

the old trees
at the pasture's edge

the
little
bird
rides
the
tall
weed
down

thumps in the night . . .
  apples dropping
     in the moonless orchard

hunter's moon –
   the cat comes home
      faintly smelling of wood smoke

away from the party din –
  Jupiter's bold shine
    among black boughs

in the dim
   of a December afternoon –
     huge snowflakes

                  wassailing –
                  so cold
                  the rum
                  can't find
                  our toes

Christmas Eve –
across
the snow hushed town
St. Mary's chimes . . .

such an affection
for this only spider –
Christmas alone

this bitter bitter night —
a wild wind warps St. Brigid's bells

dim
in driven snow

two crows
hunched

on a
white-black bough

snowbound –
me
and the woman in the painting

through bleak
branches
a white moon

on the snow
a shadow orchard

frosting the window
with our breath –
tick-tack-toe

stark
winter sky –
a hawk
completes
the tree

an essence
of summer

in the buzz
of a fly –

snowflakes
at the window

along the snow path

the clatter
of a curled leaf

rolling
with the wind

after a winter of boots
a certain spring
in my step

skunk cabbage –
putting the stiff snake
in a sunny spot

where crabapples bloom
along the avenue, we say goodbye
raspberry sherbet

listening
for the barred owl,

a moth
flutters into
my shirt

morning-glory at dusk the bee's trapped hum

summer   seen through the screen door

twilight –

bursts
of buzzing

among
the asters

crickets
chatting up
crickets

dense fog
to the north a chain saw
gnars a tune

one after the other
three crows become one
with the fog

dear fly
we can't go on like this

snow falling
    in the park at dusk . . .
       the yellow windows

on the gusty
street —

a snow ghost
pirouettes
and disappears

a quaint street scene
    painted on a tin . . .
        scent of hot cocoa

by the stone church
 in the pearly-gray sunlight
  the dogwood's pink

                              through a haze
                               of leaflets

                               the ugliest
                               gargoyle
                               ever

she loiters
smelling a spray of violets
– the nape of her neck

shying away
she leaves her sly smile
but not her name . . .

where she stood
a twist
of blue smoke   lingers
in the misting air

late sunlight
        climbs the hotel wall
                cigarette by cigarette

cruel words
the inadequacy of long-stemmed roses

stars in a black sky –
       across the river a clock
              strikes one . . . strikes two

again, the great maple
    turns Halloween orange
      again, this longing

                honking
                    a wedge of geese
                heading . . .

outlawed —
but somewhere the incense
of burning leaves

on the closed spinet
an arrangement of bittersweet,
her favorite . . .

a sudden
flush from peach
to rose

every branch
aglitter
with ice

in snow
and stony silence,
her name

graven
in
granite

where snowflakes become ocean
she takes my arm
          the cry of gulls

on my palm
      this snowflake
            swiftly becoming . . .

About the Author

Larry Kimmel was born in Johnstown, PA. He holds degrees from Oberlin Conservatory and Pittsburgh University, and has worked at everything from steel mills to libraries. Now self-employed, he lives with his wife in the hills of western Massachusetts.

To learn more about the work of Larry Kimmel see:
http://www.winfredpress.com

www.ingramcontent.com/pod-product-compliance
Lightning Source LLC
Chambersburg PA
CBHW031548040426
42452CB00006B/241